Old BUTE

by
Graham Twaddle

East Princes Street, Rothesay.

First published in the United Kingdom, 2000,
by Stenlake Publishing Ltd.
Telephone: 01290 551122
www.stenlake.co.uk

ISBN 1 84033 099 6

This book has been published in association with Bute Museum.

ACKNOWLEDGEMENTS

I would like to thank the following people for their help with this book: The Trustees of the Bute Museum for their permission to reproduce 22 photographs from their archives in the book. In particular, my thanks are due to Mrs Kathleen Clegg for her assistance, and for sharing her considerable knowledge of the island with me.

Mrs Elizabeth Johnston, a former resident of Inchmarnock, who has kindly allowed me to use a photograph from her time on the island.

Mr Malcolm Allan, Special Collections librarian at the University of Strathclyde, who unearthed some timely gems from the library's excellent Robertson Collection.

Finally, my sincere thanks to Charles and Sheila Murray of Rothesay for the use of several original photographs from their collection, and above all, for their considerable hospitality over the years.

The publishers would like to thank Robert Grieves for providing the picture of the charabanc that appears on page 29.

FURTHER READING

The books listed below were used by the author during his research. None of them are available from Stenlake Publishing. Those interested in finding out more are advised to contact their local bookshop or reference library.

Cormack, I. (1986) *The Rothesay Tramways Company, 1879-1949.*
Hamilton, Ian (1993) *Papers Relating to Andrew B. Baird (1862-1951)*
MacCallum, J. *Wish You Were Here.*
McLagan, I. (1997) *The Piers and Ferries of Bute.*
Marshall, Dorothy N. (1992) *History of Bute.*
Munro, Ian S. (1973) *The Island of Bute.*
Newton, Norman S. (1999) *The Isle of Bute.*
Shaw, Annie (ed.) (1991) *Rothesay's Yesterdays.*
The Third Statistical Account of Scotland: Renfrew and Bute (1962).
Walker, A. and Sinclair, F. (1992) *The North Clyde Estuary: an Illustrated Architectural Guide.*

INTRODUCTION

To anybody watching the modest numbers of cars and foot passengers landing at Rothesay pier during the Glasgow Fair weekend nowadays, it is hard to visualise the same scene, but with hundreds – even thousands – thronging the pier and esplanade of the town. But in its heyday as a tourist destination, from the 1880s to the early 1920s, Bute – styled 'the Madeira of Scotland' by its promoters – was perhaps closer to the modern day Mallorca or Ibiza in its sheer popularity.

Rothesay was the quintessential Clyde coast resort. During the months of July and August the population of the island (around 12,000 in the early 1900s) almost tripled. After World War II Bute's popularity waned, but the sight of queues of people – this time mainly day-trippers – during the Glasgow, Paisley and Greenock Fairs is well within living memory, persisting until the 1970s. Nowadays tourism continues to be important to the island's economy, but it is of a different nature, and today's calm and lack of bustle is more of a selling point than a disadvantage to the sort of visitor now being attracted to Bute.

As with other Clyde coast resorts, it was the moneyed and leisured classes who first discovered the charms of Rothesay. With the introduction of a steamboat service to the island in 1814, bringing it within three-and-a-half hours of Glasgow, the town became what was described as a 'fashionable watering place'. From then on it underwent continuous expansion, initiated by the wealthy mercantile classes of Glasgow who built increasingly grand summer residences along the bay. A guidebook from the 1840s heaps these praises upon the town:

> There are few places in this kingdom that combine to a greater degree the advantages of a salubrious and invigorating air, a beautiful expanse of sea, with more pleasing scenery, than this interesting town. The lover of nature, the student, or the invalid may frequent these shores with equal benefit and gratification.

At around the same time an equally extravagant claim was made for Rothesay as 'the Montpelier of Scotland'. Later the town would get the nickname 'Glasgow by the sea', less glamorous, and reflecting the change in the nature of the island's tourist industry. For in the last decades of the nineteenth century it was the working classes who made Rothesay their holiday destination, and their presence during the summer months brought a distinctly urban air to the town. The impact of this annual inundation upon the lives of the townspeople was immense, and for many it was a valuable opportunity to supplement their incomes by taking in paying guests. With accommodation scarce, even the most ordinary tenement flats were sought-after. It was not unknown for a whole family to rent and crowd into the living room or kitchen of such a flat, while the occupants removed themselves to the other room. Such conditions were endured for the sake of a fortnight by the sea, and city-dwellers paid up to £6 for the privilege. Accommodation was sometimes so scarce that families had to spend their first night sleeping out of doors. Elsewhere on the island tourism prospered too, though on a smaller scale, in Kilchattan Bay and Port Bannatyne, with day-trips to the sandy beaches of Ettrick Bay.

Of course to describe Bute solely as a holiday island is to tell only part of the story, even in this century. The Bute Museum in Rothesay gives a fascinating insight into the island's long and distinguished history. Archaeological digs across the island have unearthed evidence of human habitation as far back as 3500 BC. And Bute is dotted with standing stones and circles, still an enigmatic presence in the landscape, after almost two thousand years. Every wave of visitors and settlers has left its mark in some way, from Vikings, Celtic monks, eighteenth century industrialists, to the urban Scottish holidaymaker sailing 'doon the watter' of more recent memory.

The collection of pictures in this book combines picture postcards of Victorian and Edwardian times with more intimate, islander's-eye views of life on Bute. There have been conspicuous changes to life on the island over the last hundred years: traditional sources of employment such as tourism and agriculture have declined, the population has shrunk, and some small villages, once self-contained communities, live on only as names on maps and a few isolated houses. But just as these old photographs testify to change, they also highlight continuity. Island communities by their very nature tend to be relatively self-sufficient, and a greater variety of businesses and amenities remain in Rothesay than in many a mainland town of greater size. Likewise, a sense of community and local identity, greatly eroded in many places, is still present among the islanders. Yet unlike many Scottish islands, Bute is not isolated. Lying on the geological fault-line between the Highlands and Lowlands it enjoys the best of both worlds. To islanders it offers easy access to urban life, while for tourists its accessibility from the city makes it an ideal holiday destination.

Public transport in Bute at the turn of the century. This Rothesay-bound horse-drawn omnibus has probably come from Kilchattan Bay and Kingarth. There was little in the way of public transport on the island until the 1880s, when horse-drawn buses and trams began to cater for the growing influx of holidaymakers. Whilst Rothesay and Port Bannatyne enjoyed a tram service, the tramway was never extended as far as Kilchattan Bay, which relied on horse-drawn transport until the introduction of motor vehicles after the World War I. Horse-drawn buses such as this one were brightly painted and often driven by coachmen wearing scarlet coats and top hats. From 1899 to the mid-1930s, the main operator on this route was the local firm of McKirdy and McMillan, which once had a 29-strong fleet of buses.

Muir's bakery was founded in 1878, and had premises on Argyle Street and High Street in Rothesay, as well as shops in Port Bannatyne, Kilchattan Bay and Ardbeg. Its shortbread and meringues were particularly popular. This horse-drawn baker's van was used into the 1930s to deliver bread to the town's hotels and guest houses, as well as to some private houses. It can now be seen in Glasgow's Museum of Transport. The photograph was taken in front of the Bute Arms Hotel, which stood on Guildford Square until 1984 when it was demolished following a fire.

Ascog, essentially a suburb of Rothesay, was the address of choice for the well-to-do, and this is reflected in the increasingly grand houses and mansions that line the coast road from Rothesay. Most of the large houses were built between the mid-1800s and the 1880s for wealthy Glasgow families who would dwell there in grand style, with full retinues of servants. Many of the huge properties were subsequently divided up or converted into residential homes, such as a railway convalescent home, a Salvation Army rest home, and three schools, all of which are now private residences again. Ascog is the site of a rare Victorian fernery, carefully restored after many years of neglect, and now open to the public. The house to the right of the picture was the Agnes Patrick School, and the building above it the Stevenson Home. The middle house, St Anne's Lodge, was owned for a time by R. B. Cunningham Graham (1852-1936), writer, MP, South American adventurer and famous personality of his time.

Craigmore pier, situated on the outskirts of Rothesay, was built between 1876 and 1877. It is a reflection of the extent of traffic to the island at that time that a second pier so close to the town's main landing stage was considered financially viable. Craigmore was designed to cater exclusively for passenger traffic and was used extensively from the 1880s until World War I. Thereafter there was a gradual decline in traffic. This photograph, showing the steamer *Mercury* calling at the pier on its way to Rothesay, dates from the early 1900s. The last passenger steamer used the pier in 1939, and Craigmore was scrapped during World War II. The tennis courts in the picture are now the site of Craigmore Bowling Club, although the attractive pier buildings still remain. A mineral well once stood near the pier, which according to the Rev. Robert Craig, writing in 1845, was 'much used by invalids' who derived 'great benefit from its waters'. Another less enthusiastic writer who tasted the sulphurous waters wrote: 'We cannot advise any of our friends who are free from cutaneous disease to venture on a similar ordeal'.

East Princes Street in the early 1920s, with the Parisian-style Duncan's Halls to the right. These were also known as the New Public Halls, Assembly Halls and Palace Halls. Built in 1879 for a former provost of the town, they could be rented out for dances and other functions. The halls also served as the entrance to the Palace Cinema, which stood immediately behind them. Duncan's Halls have closed, but the apartments above are still occupied.

An early Rothesay taxi and its driver outside the taxi and bus firm of J. & A. Martin on East Princes Street. The Martin brothers' company was one of several private motor bus firms which operated on the island until the mid-1930s. Their main route was between Rothesay, Port Bannatyne and Ettrick Bay. Eventually buses proved more popular than trams, and the Rothesay Tram Company was taken over by the Western SMT bus company in 1931. They then bought out most of the independent operators on the island. The corner of the Kettledrum Tearoom – still in existence, and run for many years by the Ramacciotti family – can be glimpsed to the left of Martin's office.

Albert Place at the corner of East Princes Street and Bishop Street. The spire of Trinity Church on Castle Street can be seen in the background. The main post office (right), with its Dutch-style gable, dates from 1896. The Albert fountain, built in memory of Prince Albert in 1863, is now the site of a plain traffic island.

The corner of Albert Place looking towards Guildford Square, photographed before the First World War. The Temperance Hotel, on the corner of the square, survives as the Esplanade, but the buildings to the right of it were demolished in December 1999. The properties standing slightly back from the others on Guildford Square have also been demolished. These included the old Clydesdale Bank and the Bank of Scotland. This part of town was built on land reclaimed from the sea in the mid-nineteenth century. Before then the shoreline lay much further inland, not far from Rothesay Castle. This explains why the High Street and the Parish Church seem so far from the town centre today. Unfortunately, the seafront is vulnerable to flooding, and the last severe flood was in 1991.

Guildford Square and East Princes Street photographed in the 1880s. Guildford Square takes its name from the wife of the second Marquis of Bute, a daughter of the Earl of Guildford. The Bank of Scotland and Clydesdale Bank stood behind the Ewing Fountain. Today this area has been paved over, and the square is far more open than it was then. The two-storey buildings to the left of the Duncan Halls on East Princes Street were replaced by tenements in the early 1900s.

Rothesay pier in the early 1900s. Judging by the number of yachts in the bay, the photograph was probably taken during the annual Clyde Yachting Regatta, which took place over two weeks in July. The yachts were at their grandest in the years before World War I, and visitors to the island's shores included Sir Thomas Lipton on board the *Shamrock*, and Kaiser Wilhelm of Germany on the *Meteor*. The pier buildings in the photograph stood from 1884 to 1962, when they were destroyed by fire. In 1968 they were replaced by unappealingly designed and impractical flat-roofed buildings. These were demolished in the early 1990s. Today's pier buildings, opened in May 1992, are more attractive and take account of the original appearance of the pier. One remnant of the old pier that has survived unscathed are the famed Victorian toilets, to the far left of the picture. They opened in 1899 and were carefully restored in the 1990s. With an ornate interior of patterned ceramic tiles, mosaic floors, and original fittings, they are a fine example of Victorian civic plumbing and nowadays are as much a public attraction as a public convenience.

This photograph shows Rothesay pier in Glasgow Fair week, probably in the 1880s. The density of the crowd on the pier gives some idea of the numbers of visitors to the island at the time. At the peak of its popularity there were sometimes more than 100 steamers calling at Rothesay each day. The bandstand in the centre of the promenade was built in 1873. Standing on the hill above the town between the two churches is the old Rothesay Academy.

This rather Spartan-looking holiday camp wasn't the first such establishment on Bute (see page 17), and was one of the less expensive ways of having a family holiday. Founded by the United Co-operative Baking Society in 1911, the Co-op Camp was situated at the top of the Serpentine Road, with fine views over the bay and the town. Nowadays a caravan park occupies the site.

The Stevenson Home in Ascog was one of several such homes in the area run by Glasgow Corporation to give poor children from the city a short break by the seaside. The 'Fresh-Air Fortnight' continued into the 1970s, although by this time children's stays tended to last longer than a few days. This postcard was sent in August 1912 by a teacher who had just got home after a fortnight at Ascog looking after 40 children. 'You ought to have seen them land, and all looking so well', she remarked. As well as the Stevenson Home there was the adjoining Agnes Patrick School (Roman Catholic, for girls aged 8-15), and the non-denominational South Park school for girls, which later became a special needs school and finally closed in the 1980s.

The Healtheries was founded in 1905 and described as a 'holiday camp for ladies and gentlemen'. The regime of exercise and simple living, combined with the name of the place, implied that a stay was beneficial to the health of visitors. During the evacuation of children from Glasgow to Bute at the beginning of the Second World War, some of the more troublesome children were housed in the Healtheries, and the town clerk of Rothesay observed tartly that 'the proprietor is well up in managing this class of person'. The Healtheries was situated on the outskirts of Rothesay, just behind Skipper Wood.

Rothesay's Winter Gardens, situated on the seafront near the pier, were built between 1923 and 1924 on the site of the old bandstand. The fine iron-framed auditorium could seat up to 1,200 people and was used for concerts, theatre shows and dances. During the summer months it was home to the extremely popular 'Rothesay Entertainers': the 'F & F' are the initials of the impresarios Messrs Fyfe and Fyfe. In the Winter Gardens' heyday there were several performances an evening, with frequent changes of programme. Names of entertainers who appeared there include Charlie Kemble, Jack Anthony, Janette Adie, Peggy Desmond and Jimmy Logan. Variety-style entertainment went out of fashion in the 1960s, and the Winter Gardens went into decline, ending up as the venue for a fun fair by the 1970s. The building lay derelict for about 10 years before being rescued in the mid-1980s and refurbished at a cost of around £850,000. It now houses a small cinema, a welcome addition to the island's amenities, and a restaurant.

Community life in Rothesay and elsewhere on the island has always been very strong, and dozens of clubs and societies flourished on Bute, particularly in the winter months when an absence of visitors gave the islanders more time for leisure. The Isle of Bute Musical Association was one of several such groups on the island, and this photograph shows them performing *The Mikado* by Gilbert and Sullivan in March 1956 at the Winter Gardens. 'Many Rothesay men and women', the author of the *Third Statistical Account for Scotland* commented rather dryly, 'are firmly assured within themselves of one thing at least, namely that they are born actors, richly gifted with histrionic talent.'

The Rothesay Pavilion opened in 1938, the winning design in a competition run by the burgh council for a building to add to the town's leisure, tourist and entertainment facilities. It could be used as a concert hall, dance hall, and for theatrical performances and meetings, and had a cafe that was long popular with holidaymakers for its fish and chip lunches and high teas. The Pavilion never quite rivalled the Winter Gardens as a venue for shows, and it is as a dance hall that it will be remembered by most. It is a very fine example of art deco architecture and continues to serve a variety of purposes. The Pavilion is still considered to have one of the best dance-floors in the West of Scotland.

Rothesay's esplanade was laid out along the town's waterfront in the 1870s. For all its popularity as a resort, Rothesay has little in the way of the sandy beaches to be found elsewhere on the island: the small area pictured, known as the Children's Corner, was one of the few spots suitable for paddling. According to a guidebook to the town: 'At the Children's Corner, off the Esplanade, the young folk gather with their spades and pails to revel in the sand'. In earlier days this area served a grimmer purpose: it was the site of the town gallows.

Part of Rothesay's seafront as it appeared in the 1950s. The church is St John's, demolished in the 1970s, and the art deco style building is the Regal Cinema, built in 1938. Its closure in the early 1980s left the island without a cinema until the refurbishment of the Winter Gardens in 1990. At one time the town had as many as four cinemas: the Regal, the Ritz on High Street, the Palace (off East Princes Street), and the de Luxe on Store Lane.

Montague Street, still one of Rothesay's main shopping streets, pictured here in March 1900. The flags outside the shops are to celebrate the relief of Ladysmith during the Boer War.

A fishmonger's and poulterer's shop on the corner of Montague Street and Bridgend Street, now a newsagent's. The shop was later taken over and run for many years by Miss Annie Jeffrey. It is doubtful if today's public taste – or health and safety regulations – would tolerate so many dead animals hanging up in the open air.

Demolished in 1974, the Norman Stewart Institute stood on the corner of High Street and Montague Street. This 'recreation and reading room' was opened in 1885, a gift to the town from the estate of Norman Stewart, a Rothesay man who had emigrated to the USA. In addition to a library, there was a billiard room on the second floor, with Johnson's tearoom and restaurant on the ground floor. According to one old resident of the town, the restaurant was 'an institution in itself . . . locals could go to the back door and for a tanner [6d] could have a jug filled with home-made soup left over from the luncheons, or portions of stew'. For a while the building served as the headquarters of the Buteshire County Library service.

Built between 1843 and 1845 as a Free Kirk after the Great Disruption of the Church of Scotland, this church on Castle Street later rejoined the established church and is now known as Trinity Church. The collapse of its roof in 1907, pictured in this card, was only a temporary setback for its congregation, which is still in existence. Scottish Presbyterianism could and can be highly factional, and this tendency left Rothesay over-endowed with churches and breakaway congregations. Inevitably, as the townsfolk's zeal for churchgoing has declined, many churches have closed down and congregations merged.

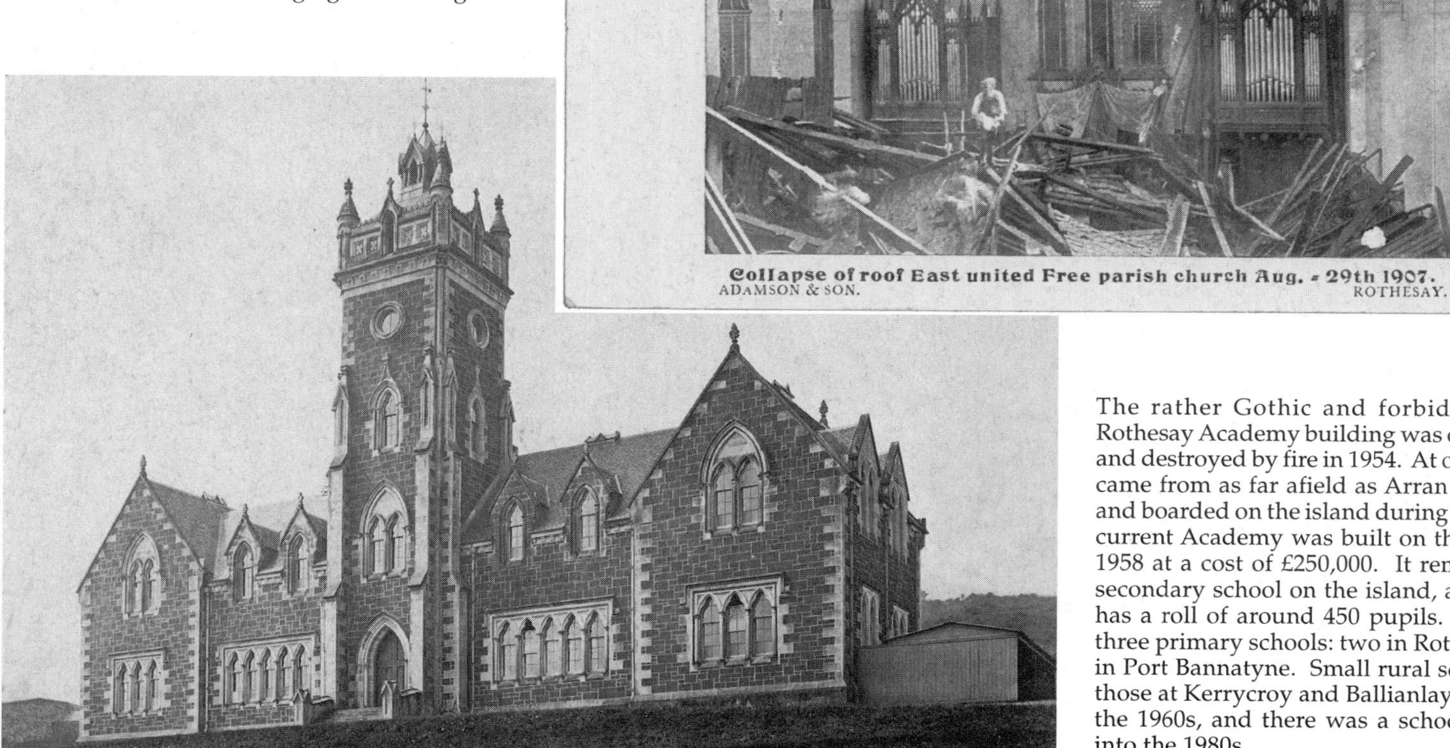

The rather Gothic and forbidding-looking Rothesay Academy building was opened in 1870 and destroyed by fire in 1954. At one time pupils came from as far afield as Arran and Cumbrae and boarded on the island during the week. The current Academy was built on the same site in 1958 at a cost of £250,000. It remains the only secondary school on the island, and nowadays has a roll of around 450 pupils. Bute still has three primary schools: two in Rothesay and one in Port Bannatyne. Small rural schools such as those at Kerrycroy and Ballianlay survived into the 1960s, and there was a school in Kingarth into the 1980s.

The staff of Rothesay steam laundry. Steam laundries caught on at the turn of the century when inefficient detergents meant that high temperatures were needed to get clothes really clean. Although much of the washing would have been done by machine, delicate garments still had to be hand washed, and the staff of this laundry would have starched and ironed clothes as well as washing them. A great deal of the steam laundry's business came from the town's many guesthouses and hotels during the summer months. The laundry stood between Ladeside Street and King Street.

Staff of *The Buteman* in the newspaper's print room. The editor, Mr Charles Stevenson, is standing second from the left in the centre row. *The Buteman* was founded in 1854 and soon became the island's established weekly source of local news. Its appearance every Thursday is still eagerly awaited by many islanders, and quite a few copies are sent abroad to expatriate islanders wanting to keep in touch with their roots. At one time Bute had as many as three newspapers: as well as *The Buteman*, there was the *Rothesay Express* which appeared midweek and ceased publication in 1953, and the *Rothesay Chronicle*, which ran until 1924.

The story of Rothesay blacksmith Andrew Baird is a footnote in the history of aviation. Born in 1862, Baird moved to Rothesay at the age of twenty-five and ran a blacksmith's business on the High Street. He was a founder of the Scottish Aeronautical Society, and having been fired with enthusiasm by a visit to an aeronautical exhibition in Blackpool in 1909, returned to his own workshop and set about trying to design his own flying machine (above). This had a wingspan of 29 feet, was constructed from iron tubes and bamboo, and was fitted with an Edinburgh-built engine to which he had attached a propeller. The flying machine was exhibited at Rothesay Highland Games in 1910, and its test flight took place in front of a crowd of spectators along the beach at Ettrick Bay later that summer. According to contemporary reports the plane did take off, but landed again shortly afterwards after swerving sharply to the right. Unfortunately, already in late middle age, Andrew Baird seems to have abandoned any further serious attempts at aviation, and died at the age of 89, a relatively unknown figure.

Small charabancs such as this model 'T' Ford were a more common means of getting round the island than home-made aeroplanes. This one was owned by McKellar of Craigmore in the 1920s, and was painted in an attractive silver livery with gold mudguards. It was photographed at Albert Pier en route to Ettrick Bay.

The remains of this sea-bathing station, with its changing rooms, lido and spectators' gallery, may still be seen along Ardbeg Road not far from Isle of Bute Sailing Club. The bathing station was popular in the late 1920s and early thirties, but when indoor heated baths were opened in the former Royal Aquarium in 1938 sea-bathing quickly lost its allure. As one local writer put it: 'Rothesay youth swims gallantly in the pond but carefully avoids the cruel sea'. The baths at the Royal Aquarium closed in the 1980s and the building has since been turned into flats. Rothesay's new public swimming pool opened on High Street in 1989.

Rothesay Tramways Company Ltd. was founded in 1879, and horse-drawn trams began running on the island in 1882. The original lines extended from Guildford Square in Rothesay to the end of Marine Road in Port Bannatyne. Trams ran half-hourly between 8.30 and 9.30 a.m., then four times an hour from 10 a.m. to 10 p.m. The journey-time between Rothesay and Port Bannatyne was about 30 minutes. In 1902 electric trams were introduced, cutting the journey-time down to 15 minutes. These were powered by a generator located in the Pointhouse Depot at Port Bannatyne. By the 1930s trams were experiencing fierce competition from buses, and after several years of declining passenger numbers the last official tram on Bute ran on Wednesday 30 September 1936.

In 1905 the tramway was extended from Port Bannatyne to Ettrick Bay, a popular destination for holidaymakers because of its fine sandy beach. The tram route was an attractive one, running through the countryside, and trams could reach a speed of 25 mph (they were restricted to 6 mph in the built up areas). Having invested in the line, the tramway company did much to popularise the route, laying on special events at Ettrick Bay such as open-air concerts, dances, and events for children. Unbelievably though, considering the island's economy depended so much on tourism, Sunday trams did not start to run until 1925, when the burgh council had to run a referendum on the issue. In spite of strong sermons against the evils of Sunday traffic from various pulpits, Sunday trams received a healthy 1,200 votes in their favour, with 549 against.

Ardbeg Road in the early 1900s. Ardbeg was the next suburb to grow up out of Rothesay after Ascog, but was described as 'slightly lower down on the social scale'. Unlike Ascog, however, Ardbeg developed a more discernible separate identity from the main town and had more shops and amenities. The house in the left foreground stands on the site of the birthplace of the eminent Scottish surgeon Sir William MacEwan (1848-1924), and a commemorative plaque marks the spot.

After Rothesay, Port Bannatyne is the island's second largest centre of population, and was home to almost 2,000 people in the 1920s (its population now stands at around 700). Port Bannatyne's main industries were herring fishing, a slate quarry and boat building (the latter is still pursued in the village). Its popularity as a resort was far more modest than Rothesay's, but many visitors passed through it during the summer months en route to the beach at Ettrick Bay. The church in the picture was St Bruoc's, destroyed by fire in the 1960s.

The rather basic-looking pier shown in this early 1900s view was built by Duncan Hoyle, Laird of Kamesburgh (the old name for Port Bannatyne) in 1857. Apparently the new amenity met with some opposition from local residents, who would have preferred their village to remain a quiet backwater. The pier was much in use until the First World War and served as the terminus for Caledonian Company steamers, as well as being the base for Captain John Williamson's three steamers – the *Sultan*, *Sultana* and *Viceroy* – known as the Turkish fleet. It was last used for scheduled traffic in 1939. During the Second World War the Hydropathic Hotel, immediately above it, was taken over by the Admiralty and the pier was used for naval traffic, and also as a base for salvage operations. Today the pier is derelict. The original hotel was built as early as 1877 but was burnt down, and the building in this picture dated from 1911. The Hydropathic was described as 'always [being] full of a better class of visitor', but closed in the 1970s.

The permanent staff of the Rothesay Tramways Company photographed at the Pointhouse Depot in Port Bannatyne. The man in the trilby hat at the centre of the group is believed to be the general manager, Archibald Robertson. There were around 6 drivers (paid 1 shilling an hour) and 6 conductors (paid 4½d. an hour), but during the summer months extra conductors – often schoolboys – were taken on to cope with the increased numbers of passengers. During the First World War women conductors were employed for the first time, and as the number of men leaving for war increased there were women tram drivers too. A number of male employees had already enlisted by the end of 1914, which would date this photograph to *c*.1915 when the first women conductors were recruited. Wartime conditions would also account for the extreme youth of some of the conductors in the front row.

The pavilion on the left was built by the tramways company and stood until 1968 when it was blown down in a January gale. It was the venue for many concerts and evening dances during the summer months, and special all-inclusive tickets to these events were sold by the tramways company for a shilling. Today a popular cafe stands on the site of the old pavilion, and the bay is still as delightfully unspoilt as it is in this early 1920s view.

E 398 Ettrick Bay

The sender of another 1920s postcard described Ettrick Bay as 'the children's paradise and joy ground of Scotland'. Apart from donkey rides – a common sight at many seaside resorts – other activities for the young included an annual sandcastle building competition, sponsored by the tramway company, and from 1936 to 1943 a mini railway.

Originally purchased by the general manager of the Western SMT Company for his son, this American-built miniature locomotive ran for several seasons at Ettrick Bay as a novelty ride. This picture was taken in 1937, and the driver of the locomotive was Angus McQueen of Port Bannatyne.

The island of Inchmarnock lies about a mile off the west coast of Bute. It is about two miles long and half-a-mile wide. Although now uninhabited and overgrown, it has a very long history of human settlement. A Bronze Age burial cist was excavated on the island by the Bute archaeologist Dorothy Marshall, and the finds, including a black jet necklace, may be seen in Bute Museum. At one time there were three farms on the island – South Park, Mid Park and North Park. This photograph shows some summer visitors to Mid Park in the 1950s. The last farmer and his family left the island in the 1980s. Inchmarnock had the nickname 'the drunkard's island' among Bute people, possibly because a few soaks were once sent there to dry out.

Another agricultural scene, this time haymaking on a farm at Kilchattan Bay in the 1930s. Farming in the Kilchattan Bay area is chiefly dairy, although the light sandy soil of this part of Bute is also suitable for potatoes, and the early crop is particularly popular. During haymaking a farm-worker's day could last from 5 a.m. to 9 or 10 p.m. According to the Rev. James Thorburn, writing in the 1790s, all the reaping in Kingarth parish was done by women.

A beached boat, probably at Ettrick or Scalpsie Bay at the turn of last century. This photograph, together with those on pages 21, 41 and 48 (left), was taken by the amateur Bute photographer James McCrone (1855-1933) who lived at Townhead, Rothesay, and ran a draper's shop in the town.

WHELK GATHERERS, KERRYCROY

With its Tudor-style houses and village green complete with maypole, the little village of Kerrycroy, about halfway between Rothesay and Kingarth, looks decidedly un-Scottish – and such was the intention. It was built on the edge of the Mount Stuart Estate between 1805 and 1806 as a model village for estate workers, and was designed in the style of an English village to remind the second Marchioness of Bute of home. At one time it had an inn, schoolroom and post office. The stone quay at Kerrycroy was once one of the island's main links with the rest of the world, with a ferry and post-boat crossing back and forth to Largs in the days before steamships.

Living rough in Bute in the 1890s. At the end of the nineteenth century there were several families of tinkers on the island who lived under canvas or animal-skin tents for much of the year. Bute also had a well-known cave-dweller called Jinty Bell, who sold cockles at Rothesay pier and lived in a cave south of Ettrick Bay. She was described as 'a small-made woman with a wizened face, light on her feet, tidy, and with an eye as bright as a bird's'. According to the same writer, her cave was 'not a pretty sight – something like the prehistoric dwellings which archaeologists unearth from time to time, and reconstruct from the remains of the middens'.

At one time the Parish of Kingarth, which comprises the villages of Kingarth and Kilchattan Bay, had a population of over 1,000. Now the figure stands at less than 400. The nearby monastery of St Blane, founded by the saint in the sixth century, made the village more important than Rothesay at one time. Gaelic was spoken in the parish well into the nineteenth century, to the pique of one English minister who thought it 'possibly to the hindrance of the more easy and more ready introduction of new methods and improvements'. In the nineteenth century there was a small tile works based at Kingarth which survived until 1915. This picture shows the schoolhouse, which closed in 1981 and is now a riding centre. The white building on the left was the village hall, which stood until the 1960s.

Shinty is still a popular game on the island, and the main shinty club is now in Rothesay, where a new clubhouse has recently been built on the Meadows.

At one time there were six alehouses in the parish of Kingarth, a number that the parish minister thought excessive and likely to prove injurious to morals. The Kingarth Hotel is now the only pub left in the village, although there is a licensed hotel in nearby Kilchattan Bay. The horse-drawn coach is McKirdy and McMillan's *Star of Bute* and is on its way to Kilchattan Bay. The journey time from Rothesay to Kilchattan Bay was about one-and-a-half hours.

Kilchattan Bay is one of several places in Scotland that takes its name from St Catan, a fifth century holy man who built a retreat for himself at this spot. Scandalised by his unmarried sister giving birth to a baby boy, he is said to have cast the child and its mother out to sea – hardly an act of Christian charity. Both survived the ordeal and safely reached the coast of Ireland, where the boy, named Blane, was taught by St Kenneth and St Comgall. Upon returning to Bute – and obviously more magnanimous than his uncle – he was also taught by St Catan himself. Blane too was made a saint and gave his name to the town of Dunblane. In spite of its local saints, the island's patron saint is Brendan, and the islanders are sometimes known as Brandanes.

The front at Kilchattan Bay has changed little since this postcard was sent in 1907. Most of the tenements date from the 1870-1885 period, when the village grew as a result of better connections with Rothesay and Glasgow and started to become popular. The bay once had a post office, drapers, bakery, greengrocers, cafe and a summer tearoom. Not all visitors to the bay have been charmed, however, and in 1857 the travel writer Hugh MacDonald, who managed to effuse about most places, wrote: 'We do not find it particularly attractive. The amenities of the regular watering place are, in a great measure, awanting'.

This stone quay was built at Kilchattan Bay in the 1820s and still stands, having been refurbished in 1990 by the Kingarth and Kilchattan Bay Improvement Committee. A steamer pier was opened in 1880, and services ran from Kilchattan Bay until 1955. The journey to Glasgow, via Fairlie, took about an hour and a half. One of the last vessels of any note to use the pier was the Royal Yacht *Britannia* on the occasion of the Queen's visit to the island in 1958. The pier was demolished in 1976, and today only the pier houses remain.

A local rabbit-catcher photographed with his spoils in the 1890s. Rabbits are not thought to have been brought to the island until about 1835 when they were introduced for sporting purposes. Their rapid increase in number led one author to comment that 'it would appear to be the rabbit that has had the sport'.

At the other end of the social spectrum, the fourth Marquis and Marchioness of Bute, from a postcard sent in 1906. The Bute family still owns much of the island.